THE BRITISH AT HOME

" *Why of course, Mrs. Harrison, it's* perfectly *all right about bringing with you your sister* and *her husband* and *their daughter* and *their two sons* and *their son's friend who have arrived unexpectedly.*"

THE BRITISH AT HOME

BY

PONT

WITH AN APPRECIATION

BY

T. H. WHITE

COLLINS · PALL MALL · LONDON
1939

THIS BOOK IS SET IN FONTANA, A NEW TYPE FACE
DESIGNED FOR THE HOUSE OF COLLINS, AND
PRINTED BY THEM IN GREAT BRITAIN

FIRST IMPRESSION   -   -   SEPTEMBER 1939
SECOND   ,,   -   -   DECEMBER 1939

CONTENTS

AN APPRECIATION

NOWADAYS you can do two kinds of funny pictures. Either you can do the Peter Arno kind, which consists of a top-speed pen-and-ink wash with a cute caption, or you can do the Fougasse kind, which depends on outline.

But in the old days there was a different sort of artist. There was Breughel, whose pictures needed a magnifying glass, and there was Hogarth, whose careful details kept one pondering over the significance of a crumpled bill or a broken glass, and there were the great Victorian masters of minutiæ: Phiz, Leech and Tenniel. These ancient worthies were content to spend a long time over a picture, and the curious effect was that the people who looked at the picture were content to spend a long time looking. Pont is of this school. An industrious man of regular habits, who locks himself up every day to draw, this great *Punch* artist never finishes a picture in less than a day—and the actual drawing takes a day, exclusive of working up the idea and the preliminary sketches.

The first thing you must be ready for in Pont is the detail. He is Hogarthian about it. You must be ready to turn the picture upside down in order to read the name of a book on the floor, or to examine the subjects of all the pictures on the walls: you must notice the ornaments in the room. Look at the haunted room on page sixty-six, for instance: the lady with the head under her arm, and the executioner, and the funereal plumes on the four-poster, and the suit of armour ready to pounce, and the agonised curtains and the miserable little lamp. You will see these at once. But do you see the bat, and the horribly receptive chair ? Do you see the Something coming in at the door ? What it can be, we are not intended to know. "Good-bye, sir," says the butler, and leaves us at that.

The second thing about Pont is his interest in character. I complimented him once upon his sense of humour, and he was very angry. He said: "I do not try to draw funny people. I have no sense of humour. I try very hard to draw people exactly as they are." This, of course, is why he is funny. He has no stock comic characters, no paltry little set of people with five or six expressions. He is drawing real people all the time, painfully and conscientiously observing them with the unsmiling eye, and, because all people are frightfully funny if you really look at them, he is a great comic artist. Another result is that all the people are different.

Look, for example, at the family group on page

nineteen. The Country Folk are evidently posing for a photograph in the *Tatler*. But who are they, and what sort of person would each be to meet ? My belief is that the pater-familias is going to be a governor-general—hence the photograph for the *Tatler*—and that he will be a good one. He does not understand very much, dear fellow, for he has had a sound classical education at Harrow (yes, Harrow : you would have thought Eton, but look at the tie) and his family mottoes show the extent of his learning. They are *Mensa, Mensa, Mensam* and *Palam, Clam, Cum Ex and E.* No doubt he is interested in pigs or roses. His eldest son in the riding boots is at Oxford, and he does not understand very much about things either, for he has inherited his father's eyes. I doubt if he is even good at polo. His wife was an actress, or else a famous debutante, for she still considers herself a reigning beauty and spends all the time making herself up. She is not baffled, like her husband, but simply idiotic. Like all reigning beauties, she is untidy and a nuisance to the servants, for it is my guess that it was she, and not her Oxford son, who threw that cigarette-end into the middle of the picture before assuming her oafish smile. Is there some lip-stick on it ? Next come the smaller children and the dogs. The eldest daughter is at the difficult age, poor child : she looks gawky in her jodhpurs

7

and is only half-way to her mother's appreciation of the importance of photographs. To the youngest daughter, however, I am afraid the *Tatler* is but a closed book. Whether she has seen an earwig or some private fancy we cannot tell. The second son has been birds'-nesting. They were lucky enough to catch him for the picture, and stood him there, but there was not time to brush his hair. He waits until it is over, and will be off again as soon as it is. Meanwhile he remains quiescent and without thought, with some faint forecast of the blank paternal eye. The youngest boy is the interesting one. He has had his hair safely brushed by Nannie in the nursery, and has been delivered into his mother's theatrical embrace. Observe how his behind sticks out, and with what an internal convulsion he glares upon the photographer. He does not know what the devil they are all doing. What phobias, what indignant conclusions he will arrive at in this infant crisis, we can only guess.

So far the Family, but there is still the house and the extraordinary statuary : there is still the dachshund living its own life and the gardener in the background doing heaven knows what with his straw hat. Perhaps it is not a gardener, but an uncle. If so, there may be a strain of madness at the Manor House.

I am afraid I have outstayed my welcome in this

preface, but just look for a moment's contrast at that other sinister party on page forty-five. What is happening in the family portraits ; what are the relationships between these people out of Edgar Allan Poe; which of them is mad, which doting, which neurotic, which evil, and which has long ago decided to ignore the whole situation; why the fork is bent, and what may be the nameless horror which is coming out of the soup tureen—these are a few of the delicious problems which I must now leave to the wise purchaser of this occult book.

T. H. WHITE.

FOREWORD

CLOSE observers will scarcely fail to notice that some
of the drawings in this book have been printed
"sideways." This has been done with a purpose.
People complained that the drawings in my other
book "The British Character" were for the most
part invisible to the naked eye. They asked that my
next should be larger. It was irritating, they said,
to have to employ powerful magnifying glasses
and telescopes in order to find out what was going
on. I brought my full weight therefore to bear upon
the publisher to persuade him to entertain the idea
of a larger book. He was not persuaded. However,
a compromise was reached. By printing some of
the drawings "sideways" it has been possible to
make them larger, thereby I hope pleasing the
artistic though at the cost I fear, of upsetting the
practical who will find the arrangement awkward
and will complain that it is inartistic book pro-
duction.

And that, I think, is all I have to say.

PONT.

THE BRITISH AT HOME

A. R. P. DEPT.
*" I feel sure we could drive a fire
engine."*

AT HOME
The Cricket Enthusiast

"I wonder if you realise, Wilson, that this egg is too lightly boiled."

AT HOME
The Epicure

AT HOME
The Happy Farmer

AT HOME
Country Folk

" Please don't disturb yourselves, my good people. My friend and I are only studying conditions among the rich."

AT HOME
The Millionaire

AT HOME
The Bachelor

AT HOME
The Neurotic

" Please, something which won't make me think."

AT HOME
The Author

27

AT HOME
The Fag

AT HOME
The Film Star

"... *and this time it vanished quite*
slowly, beginning with the end of the
tail, and ending with ..."

ALICE IN WONDERLAND

AT HOME
Genius

AT HOME
The Amateur Inventor

34

AT HOME
The Successful Doctor

35

AT HOME
The Singer

THE WOMAN AT HOME

*" Watch closely now, Janet, and see how I turn out a
blancmange."*

Butcher's Ounces.

38

"*Sir Thomas and Lady Partingdale, Lord Crodleigh and the Bishop of Hopton.*"

DOMESTIC DIFFERENCE.

*" Go and find the General, Peters, and tell him that if he doesn't
come in to lunch instantly he shan't have any."*

43

"*I am ever so sorry, but Mrs. Tweedie never touches soups.*"

" Crackers, Russell, for Mr. Davidson."

45

"Oh, for lunch, *was it?"*

"*Mr. Sparks, dear* . . . longing *to meet you.*"

" Now, now, your ladyship, remember the time-table—Kissing from 5.30 to 6."

48

Half-an-hour's rest after meals.

*" I hope you remembered about the shops not opening
again until Tuesday when you ordered the things in,
Madam."*

"*I don't wish to seem to be interfering or anything Mildred, but do you not think perhaps you've got your oven a wee bit high?*"

THE MAN AT HOME (and elsewhere)

" . . . and the taxpayers will shoulder
these new burdens with light hearts,
thereby showing the world, etc.,
etc., etc."

" *Of course I* entirely *agree with you. But which crisis is it you mean?*"

CONVERSATION PIECE

" Coo! Look, Sir, ain't it lovely? "

" *And here's one of him taken at Eastbourne when he was five.*"

" *Just talk to me on any subject—except hunting.* "

*" There's a most unusual-looking bird
on the lawn."*

"*I feel we should wait before making any decisions until we see what Hitler's next move is going to be.*"

" *At least, Sir, you can scarcely deny that dictators are human beings.*"

" *Did I really understand you, Miss Wilson, to use the expression,
' A cosy nook ' in connection with the house you wish me to
design for you?*"

" And now, Harrison, kindly tell cook to come up and see me for a moment."

" Good-bye, Sir."

66

" Herbert, don't disturb your Father!"

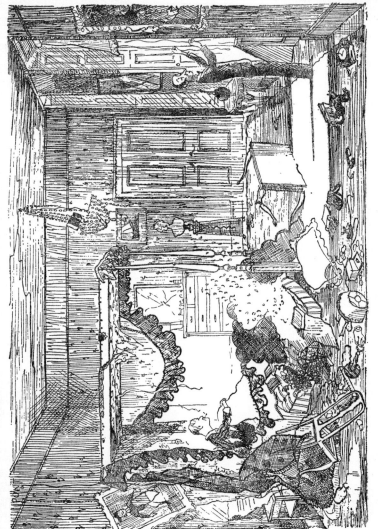

" Another restless night, Stevens."

69

" Will you please repeat that there
last remark, Mister?"

"Are you for or against Chamberlain's policy?"

"*That's not the worst; you should see
what's happened upstairs.*"

CHILDREN'S HOUR

"*But* you *weren't always
being worried to death by
war talk when* you *were
my size.*"

" Mummy, before any one invented
trains, did you——"

" *And now in return we want you to* promise *to bring all your family to spend the day with us on Saturday week.*"

"Bring her another duck, waiter."

" Master George would prefer rice-pudding."

Did you say chocolate éclair OR meringue?"

The "Please, Mother, will you tell me a story?" peril.

" I am sure none of you boys are responsible
for putting the frogs in Matron's bed last
night."

" *I'm sorry, Miss Heslop, but your Botany Hour always seems to sap my vitality.*"

" If you take my advice you won't go upstairs to her.
There's nothing wrong; she's only crying because she
just wants someone to go and talk to her."

"*I* insist *on my children always sleeping with the windows open.*"

83

" *Once upon a time there was a teeny-*
weeny little fairy . . ."

" *Now don't go walking in all those pools, Penelope,*
there's a good girl."

THE BRITISH CHARACTER

"*Ne te fâches pas, mon vieux. C'est un Anglais. Il ne peut pas nous comprendre.*"

THE BRITISH CHARACTER

PREDILECTION FOR WEEK-END COTTAGES

THE BRITISH CHARACTER

A TENDENCY TO LEAVE THE WASHING UP TILL LATER

THE BRITISH CHARACTER
A DISINCLINATION TO GO ANYWHERE

THE BRITISH CHARACTER
A TENDENCY TO BE CONSCIOUS OF DRAUGHTS

THE BRITISH CHARACTER
LACK OF CONFIDENCE IN THE DRIVER

THE BRITISH CHARACTER
A TENDENCY TO PUT OFF TILL THE LAST MINUTE

THE BRITISH CHARACTER
The tendency among week-end guests to leave things
behind

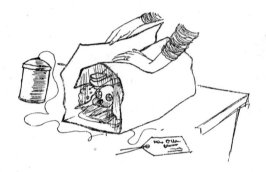

THE BRITISH CHARACTER
A TENDENCY NOT TO RETURN BORROWED BOOKS

THE BRITISH CHARACTER
Curiosity

THE BRITISH CHARACTER
Importance of not taking precedence at doorways

"Is there anything *nice in it this morning?"*

THE BRITISH CHARACTER
THE IMPORTANCE OF NEWS

THE BRITISH CHARACTER
ABILITY TO MANAGE FOR ONESELF ON SUNDAY EVENING

Sunday night supper

THE BRITISH CHARACTER
ATTITUDE TOWARDS SUNDAY MORNINGS

THE BRITISH CHARACTER
A TENDENCY TO DESPAIR ON MONDAY MORNINGS

" It's not a bit of use asking me, my dear man; I can't
see a thing."

PONT

THIS IS MR. CLOTHESBRUSH—

AND MISS THOMSON—

AND PROFESSOR CHURCHUR, WHO
INVENTED THE CHURCHUR—

AND CAPTAIN ELEPHANTSARE-
BIGTODAY—

III

AND MISS VINCENT—

AND MISS CARTER—

AND LADY HEIGH-HO—

AND MY BROTHER—

AND SIR WILLIAM GLOBBGLOB, THE FAMOUS GLOSHSUSH—

AND MY OTHER BROTHER—

AND MISS THOMSON—

AND MISS TURNEDOUTATSLOUGH (I EXPECT YOU SAW HER IN "SEVEN NINES ARE EIGHTY-FOUR")—

AND THE DEAN OF WHYNOT-
ARRESTHER—

AND OF COURSE MY MOTHER—

AND MR. PASSDOWNTHECAR-
PLEASE, WHOM YOU MET LAST
TIME—

AND NOW I'M *sure* YOU WOULD
LIKE SOMETHING TO DRINK

A HYMN OF HATE.

ADDRESSED TO MR. BROWN, MY GARDENER.

In the broad herbaceous bed,
Almost standing on his head,
Brown the gardener tends the plants.
Gently to himself he chants :
Songs of triumphs and of woes—
At the horticultural shows—
Shows of long ago when he

Took the cup for celery—

Songs of prizes he has won,
Songs of rain and songs of sun,
Songs of spades and songs of barrows
Songs of huge prize-winning marrows,
Songs of very large cucumbers,
Songs of veges without numbers.
In his thoughts there is no room
For a single flower bloom;

So in all my flower beds
Lettuce grow in giant heads,
Leek and artichoke abound
In the neatly tended ground;
Runner beans in serried ranks,
Sprouting broccoli in banks,
Peas and beet in endless rows—
Every garden herb that grows.

Now through all my house you'll find
Garden herbs of every kind
Fixed in vase and bowl and pot.
I hate my gardener quite a lot!

"*Not eating your fat—and* millions *starving in Russia!*"

" We have it in stock all right, Madam,
but it's on the top shelf."